May the sale always be with you

2/07

MAY THE SALE BE WITH YOU

START SELLING IN THE **NOW!**

RICH LUCIA

Copyright © 2008 by Richard J. Lucia.
Published by Rich Lucia.com.

All rights reserved. No part of this book may be reproduced without written permission from the publisher, except by a reviewer who may quote brief passages in a review; nor may any part of this book be stored in a retrieval system, or transmitted in any form or by any means— electronic, mechanical, photocopying, recording, or other— without written permission from the publisher.

Cover Design and Interior Design:
MacGraphics Services

Printed in the United States of America.

Lucia, Richard J. Lucia.
May the Sale be With You / Rich Lucia
ISBN: 978-0-9801547-0-2

Library of Congress Cataloguing-in-Publication Data

Dedicated to my son, Alex:

May you always seek the knowledge that will become the driving force of your life.

Dad

About this Book

It was late one September when my son, Alex, graduated in Pennsylvania and moved to Florida. He'd always been ambitious, blessed with talent and the desire to work hard. Eager to earn a buck or two, he'd ventured into several businesses in high school—delivering newspapers, working as a bus boy, and waiting tables at first. He took his earnings and bought a power washer so he could wash neighbors' driveways and decks. Then he developed another business on e-Bay by buying young tree seedlings and selling them across the country.

Alex was never big on taking direction from others. However, his personal determination served him well. I have watched him overcome every setback he'd encountered and use it as a learning experience. But I was concerned.

Alex never spent much time reading books. Instead, he leaned on the Internet to get a broad-brush view of a topic of interest. His independent, almost-a-know-it-all persona fueled my concern. I asked him why I rarely saw him reading a book. He responded with, "Dad, I can't. I can't do anything for more than ten minutes. I have ADD."

"How do you know?" I asked.

"I saw all the symptoms on a TV show. I *know* I have them all," he replied.

Now, I had observed him exploring the Internet for hours and also watch six episodes of *The Sopranos* on TV back to back, so I was sure he had the ability to concentrate. When I pointed that out, he responded with, "If you love me you would have me tested." So I called his bluff. "Alex, you can't take the test because it lasts an hour."

Nonetheless, it was clear Alex liked to "sip" on information rather than "gulping" it whole. When he told me he wanted to start a sales career and asked for my help, I was pleased and proud. After devoting more than 30 years to sales, I consider it to be the best profession in the world. To help him, though, I knew that sending him a bibliography of my sales library would be a lost cause.

How could I pass on my sales knowledge in a way that Alex—and other busy salespeople—could follow?

I knew I had to keep my messages short and to the point. I also wanted to solicit interaction. So I created a series of sales emails for Alex to "sip" from. The result is this quick information resource that encapsulates the *force* that makes a salesperson successful. With it comes my wish for every reader to enjoy "Selling in the NOW" with great success.

May the sale be with you.

Rich Lucia

Table of Contents

You've Got mail 1
The 180 Rule 13
Selling in the NOW 29
Look for the Pain, Find the Gain 53
Question and Listen 65
Prospecting 81
Ride Your Own Order Cycle 99
Who Is the Other Guy? 111
When It's Your Turn to Speak 125
You Are What You Eat 137
Conquering Objections 155
Almost the Decision Maker 183
Win Reports 201

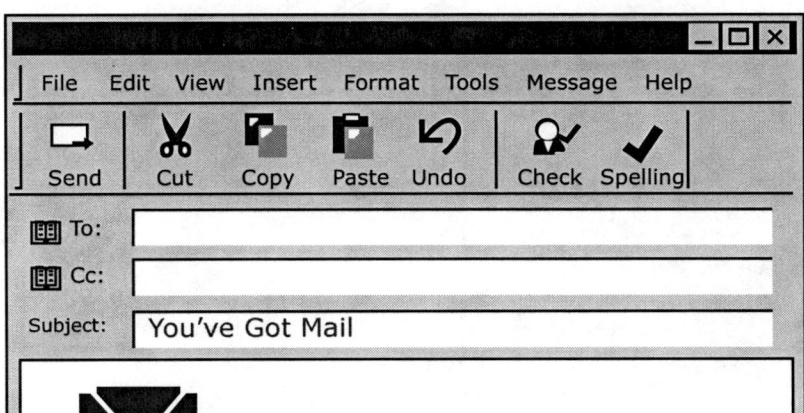

From: Alex@Intecostel.com
To: Rich@RichLucia.com
Subject: Florida's great
CC:

Dear Dad,

It's great here in Florida. The weather is hot and I love it. So do the alligators and the mosquitoes. I don't miss the cold—but I do miss the Philly cheese steaks at Pat's back home.

Great news, Dad. I decided to go into sales. If a career in sales was good enough for my dad, then it's good enough for me.

I'll keep you posted.

Alex

From: Rich@RichLucia.com
To: Alex@Intecostel.com
Subject: Good luck, son
CC:

Dear Alex,

I am glad to hear you're happy in Fort Myers, but you know, the door is always open and so is Pat's Steaks.

Good news to hear you decided on a career. Whatever you do, you know I'm behind you. Of course, I *am* partial to sales; it's been my life. I'm happy you've chosen that path.

One question: **Why Sales?**

Dad

From: Alex@Intecostel.com
To: Rich@RichLucia.com
Subject: Show me the money
CC:

Dad,

THE MONEY. That's it, the money.

Alex

From: Rich@RichLucia.com
To: Alex@Intecostel.com
Subject: Hold on there, Jerry McGuire
CC:

Alex,

No doubt you'll reap great financial rewards in sales if you perform well. But your focus needs to be on *performing well,* not on money for money's sake.

You can only be good at something if you have a desire and a passion for what you do. Earning money comes at the end of the road. Money is the natural reward as you travel the road. There's no meaningful journey without integrity, customer caring, understanding human nature, and a love for solving people's problems.

The financial rewards will come, son. I suggest you focus on what you'll be doing day after day. If you don't love what you do, you won't be able to be successful in a complete way.

Dad

From: Alex@Intecostel.com
To: Rich@RichLucia.com
Subject: Blah - Blah
CC:

Dad,

I know you teach all that stuff. But, Dad, I'm a *natural* at sales. Everyone says I'm a fabulous talker. I'll do great. I know it. So, please don't waste any of your training pitches on me. I already "get it."

Alex

From: Rich@RichLucia.com
To: Alex@Intecostel.com
Subject: Hey, smart ass
CC:

Alex,

Don't make me use CAPITAL LETTERS on you!

You were always the smart ass who could sit on a lollipop and tell what flavor it is. But this is the real deal. A lot of people tell you that ". . . you should go into sales because you're a good talker." That couldn't be further from the truth.

A great salesperson is a strong *listener*. How else can you find out what your customers really care about and what they're willing to buy?

Make sure that when you're out there, you *listen*. That's why you were given two ears and one mouth—so you'll listen twice as much as you talk. And when you *do* speak, 75% of that time you should be asking questions to give you the opportunity to listen *more*.

Get it?

Dad

From: Alex@Intecostel.com
To: Rich@RichLucia.com
Subject: Selling just isn't that hard!
CC:

Dad,

Didn't mean to get you riled up. But I've sold lots of stuff before and, frankly, selling just isn't that hard. Everyone makes a big deal about sales training.

You either have the gift to sell or you don't. What's there to learn?

Alex

From: Rich@RichLucia.com
To: Alex@Intecostel.com
Subject: Knowledge IS power
CC:

Alex,

When I was about ten, I remember a washing machine repairman came to our home. Our washer was making a terrible banging sound. Your grandmother and grandfather hoped it could be fixed easily.

The repairman listened to the clunky sound, removed a small door on the side of the washer, reached in, and tightened a screw. The sound disappeared. Then he presented your grandmother with a bill for $10, which was about what your grandfather earned in a day at that time.

Astonished at the high price, she asked, "Ten dollars to tighten one screw?" "No," he replied. "I charged 5 cents to tighten the screw. I charged $9.95 to know which screw to tighten." Right then, I recognized this truth: knowledge is power. More than that, knowledge is *profitable*.

I'm here to help you expand your knowledge, Alex, but I can only teach you what you're willing to learn.

Dad

From: Alex@Intecostel.com
To: Rich@RichLucia.com
Subject: Not as easy as selling trees at Christmas
CC:

Dad,

So far, it's not going too well. I'm making lots of sales calls, but no one is buying. My manager tells me not to be too concerned. He says, "Sales is a numbers game. Just make more calls and you will sell more."

Whatta ya think?

Alex

From: Rich@RichLucia.com
To: Alex@Intecostel.com
Subject: Numbers game
CC:

Alex,

Not so. Selling is a focused effort and should never be confused with quantity of sales calls versus quality. Here's a story that shows what I mean.

Two men were buying watermelons in the country for $1.00 apiece and selling them in the city for $1.00 apiece. This went on for weeks until one turned to the other and said, "We are selling lots of watermelons but we aren't making any money." The other said, "I know what the problem is. We need a bigger truck."

Remember, the definition of insanity is doing the same thing over and over (selling watermelons at the same price), yet expecting a different outcome (making more money).

You know, son, I can help you more if you tell me more about what's really going on.

Dad

From: Alex@Intecostel.com
To: Rich@RichLucia.com
Subject: Trying *everything*
Cc:

Dad,

Here's what's going on.

I'm cold calling, direct mailing, sending email blitzes—but nothing's working. I'm pissed! I'm pissed! I am using all these sales tools and nothing's working.

Alex

From: Rich@RichLucia.com
To: Alex@Intecostel.com
Subject: Sales tools
Cc:

Alex,

A carpenter has hundreds, no thousands, of tools to use. So does a salesperson. All your tools should be worn like a tool belt and taken out at the right time in the right situation.

Too often, I've watched salespeople stack their sales tools on top of each other. They try one after another, hoping to find the right tool that brings the right results.

But you can't drive a nail with a screwdriver any more than you can send an email campaign to someone who gets 101 emails a day. Decide first what your objective is and then pick the right tool to live by.

Dad

From: Alex@Intecostel.com
To: Rich@RichLucia.com
Subject: What's the right tool?
Cc:

Dad

But how do I know which sales tool to use when— and how do I know when I am using the wrong one? What tools should I live by?

Alex

From: Rich@RichLucia.com
To: Alex@Intecostel.com
Subject: Try this!
Cc:

Alex,

I say try the "180 Rule" as often as you can.

Let me explain it. First decide what you're trying to accomplish and then turn it around 180 degrees. To do that, make a list of what you would do if you were trying to accomplish the *exact opposite* of your original goal. Then take a look at that list. If you see activities on the list that you're currently doing, chances are you're on the wrong track. Stop doing them!

Dad

From: Alex@Intecostel.com
To: Rich@RichLucia.com
Subject: 180 degrees
Cc:

Dad,

I don't get it. Why would I want to focus on the *opposite* of what I really want?

Alex

From: Rich@RichLucia.com
To: Alex@Intecostel.com
Subject: 180 Rule
Cc:

Alex,

For some reason, people can come up with and recognize a negative action faster than they can a positive one.

Sometimes people use tools or processes because they exist rather than because they truly understand what they're trying to accomplish.

In sales, many of the same tools have been used for years, and salespeople grab at them with a "let's try this one" mentality.

The "180 Rule" is different. It's a test to see if the tool you choose really matches your goal.

Dad

From: Alex@Intecostel.com
To: Rich@RichLucia.com
Subject: The 180 thing
Cc:

Dad,

Is this one of those sales things that you teach?

Alex

From: Rich@RichLucia.com
To: Alex@Intecostel.com
Subject: Not just a sales thing
Cc:

Alex,

Yes, I speak about the "180 Rule" to help businesspeople see that, although they believe they're taking action, sometimes their action will get them the exact opposite result of what they want.

It's not just a *sales* thing; it's a *life* thing.

Do you remember the night I came home and found you watching TV instead of studying for your final? I lost it. I yelled, "GET IN THERE AND STUDY!"

Now, using the "180 Rule," what would I have said if I *didn't* want you to go in and study?

Get it?

Dad

From: Alex@Intecostel.com
To: Rich@RichLucia.com
Subject: I remember
Cc:

Dad,

I remember that. You were really mad. And I was more upset about getting caught than not studying. But to use the "180 Rule," you should have said, "Is there anything I can do to help you with your final tomorrow?"

For the record, Dad, I went in my room but never did study.

Alex

From: Rich@RichLucia.com
To: Alex@Intecostel.com
Subject: Look around you
Cc:

📎 Attachment: "180 Rule" Needed Here

Alex,

I knew you weren't studying, but I just grabbed at the first thing that popped into my head - a negative message.

Take a look around and you'll see a ton of cases when the "180 Rule" would help. Make sure you put your actions to the test—before spending a lot of time running in the wrong direction.

Dad

BTW, running faster and making more calls using the wrong tools won't work. Check some examples in this attachment.

📎 180 Rule Needed Here

Example 1:

Go into a restaurant where you are sure the owner's goal is to get repeat business by pleasing his customers. Now apply the "180 Rule." What can the restaurant do to _not_ please or delight their customers? Maybe they can:

- *Keep people waiting at the front door with a clear view of open tables as the hostess plays the "Whose table turn is it?" game.*
- *Hire wait staff that have bad attitudes. When they interact with the customers, they set up a bad experience at the table.*

Example 2:

Go to a checkout counter in a store where you can tell that the owner wants you to return and make more purchases. Does he or she convey a feeling that "we care about you and thank you for your business"?

Now apply the "180 Rule." What can the checkout people do to show a *lack of appreciation* and respect for you and your business?

Maybe they can:

- *Talk on the phone to a friend and ignore you.*
- *Sip on a drink and talk to another employee.*
- *Not make eye contact or smile.*
- *Count the cash in the register while you stand there waiting.*

The 180 Rule

- *Determine your objective.*
- *State the opposite of your objective.*
- *Develop an action list to accomplish your new objective.*
- **If anything you're doing is on that list, you're probably on the wrong track.**

One company had a sales compensation plan that allegedly was written to motivate and retain sales representatives. Then the managers applied the "180 Rule" to their plan. They listed what the plan would be like if it were written to accomplish the opposite—to demotivate the sales force and push them away.

Doing this uncovered the fact that the company was actually capping commissions, changing territories quarterly, and making no mention of a sales career path—all items noted on their list of what not *to do!*

From: Alex@Intecostel.com
To: Rich@RichLucia.com
Subject: OK, I'm lost
Cc:

Dad,

These days, I just don't even know where to begin. It seems like each day I get further behind—and this quota thing I've got hanging over my head isn't making life any easier. My company has a good product but why isn't anyone buying it?

Alex

From: Rich@RichLucia.com
To: Alex@Intecostel.com
Subject: Let's go back to the beginning
Cc:

Alex,

Before you can sell to someone, you have to get a handle on what it feels like to be a prospect in today's market—in the NOW. A majority of prospects view a traditional salesperson as a nuisance, an interruption. And why shouldn't they? People like to buy the things they perceive to need or want. However, they don't want to be forced into anything they *don't* want.

Want to see what I mean? Go to a car dealership. Walk into the showroom, make quick eye contact with a salesperson, then look away as you turn toward a car on the floor and away from the salesperson. Continue to look at the car and you can almost feel that salesperson approach. As he or she gets closer to you, the feeling you now have is what many prospects feel when they get approached. I call it the "prospect pounce."

The first job of a salesperson is to reduce or alleviate that feeling of being pounced on!

Dad

From: Alex@Intecostel.com
To: Rich@RichLucia.com
Subject: Yeah, right. Nice assignment!
Cc:

Dad,

I was already feeling bad about getting rejected out there. This "going to the car showroom" thing isn't exactly what I need to make me want to get out more often.

Besides, my manager says, "Just bang on more doors."

Alex

From: Rich@RichLucia.com
To: Alex@Intecostel.com
Subject: Banging on more doors
Cc:

Alex,

That "just bang on more doors" approach is a lot like standing at they edge of the woods, taking a shot, and hoping an animal runs into it. That's not hunting, that's shooting in the woods.

It reminds me of a famous bank robber who eluded police for years. He robbed bank after bank and still managed to avoid capture—until the day he got apprehended. A group of phychologists was asked to analyze him to find out how the criminal mind works. In theory, if they knew why, they could dissuade others from following in his footsteps. So they asked the bank robber, "Why do you rob banks?" Without hesitation, he replied, "'Cause that's where the money is."

Translated, that means *go where your customers are*.

Dad

From:	Alex@Intecostel.com
To:	Rich@RichLucia.com
Subject:	They're not getting it
Cc:	

Dad,

I am going where potential customers are. But my prospects just aren't getting it. They're not buying. I know my product and I know my company, but these *prospects* are still not getting it. Maybe I'm not pushing hard enough.

Alex

From: Rich@RichLucia.com
To: Alex@Intecostel.com
Subject: Change the title of salesperson
Cc:

Alex,

It's not about pushing hard enough, son. I think it's unfortunate that people are given the title of salesperson. Instead, we should be called *buying guides*. People love to buy, but really hate to be sold.

A forced sale is hardly ever repeated and often gets cancelled after the strong-armed pitch is a day old. It's more important to learn about your customer than learn a bunch of quick spins to persuade a prospect to buy from you.

Knowing your customer has always been important; however, the tools designed decades ago were for customers *then*.

To relate to customers today, you have to learn to "Sell in the NOW."

Dad

From: Alex@Intecostel.com
To: Rich@RichLucia.com
Subject: "Selling in the NOW"
Cc:

Dad,

What does "Selling in the NOW" mean?

Alex

From: Rich@RichLucia.com
To: Alex@Intecostel.com
Subject: New times and new customer motivations
Cc:

Alex,

"Selling in the NOW" means if you want to make a sale to today's buyers, you have to be aware of how they buy today.

Customers are definitely different from years ago. A lot of selling concepts fit for the people who were totally loyal to their jobs and company. The company's pain was their pain. Little else mattered. That's when most people stayed with their company for their entire career. They never saw massive downsizing and indiscriminate reductions in the workforce. In their world, when a layoff took place, the company stock went down. It was a sign of trouble. In contrast, a layoff today signals lower costs and higher profits, resulting in stock prices being driven up.

Take a close look at the tools you're being taught and make sure they're suited for NOW.

Dad

From: Alex@Intecostel.com
To: Rich@RichLucia.com
Subject: Wait a minute
Cc:

Dad,

Are you saying that today's buyers and customers don't care about their companies?

Alex

From: Rich@RichLucia.com
To: Alex@Intecostel.com
Subject: Company loyalty and personal priorities
Cc:

Alex,

I'm not saying that customers aren't loyal and devoted to their companies as much any more. Different priorities are now in the forefront of all prospective customers' minds.

Here's an example. You may have a product that relieves your prospect's pain and would solve a major company problem. However, if your solution requires that the buyer stays after work two extra hours a day for three months, watch out. It might conflict with what he perceives as his gain, which is getting home for dinner each night.

Go ahead and uncover the pain. But you also have to find the gain or you won't make the sale.

Dad

From: Alex@Intecostel.com
To: Rich@RichLucia.com
Subject: All bad?
Cc:

Dad,

Wait a minute. It seems to me that my sales training here has been great—filled with ideas that have been proven over and over again. Are you saying that it's all bad and I should be learning a new way?

Alex

From: Rich@RichLucia.com
To: Alex@Intecostel.com
Subject: Not bad at all
Cc:

Alex,

You just made the point that these tools are proven over time. And you're right. They haven't changed. However, the *prospects* have.

As an example, there's little demand today for a 26-page boilerplate proposal. People want their information fast, to the point, and on demand. And today, direct mail pieces find their way to the trash can faster than to the decision makers. No, the tools aren't bad. But they definitely need updating. Doing spam email blitzes has introduced an electronic aggravation and makes discarding the sales approach even easier.

Again, apply the "180 Rule." Let's say you *didn't* want your prospect to learn about your product. You can send a direct mail piece. You can send them lots of emails. You can give them a one-size-fits-all PowerPoint presentation. Or you can opt not to take the time to respond to a request. Get my point? Remember, today's customers look for the *gain*.

Dad

From: Alex@Intecostel.com
To: Rich@RichLucia.com
Subject: What's good *now*?
Cc:

Dad,

If times have changed and customers have changed, then what exactly do I need to know about the new tools for selling to the customers of today?

Alex

From: Rich@RichLucia.com
To: Alex@Intecostel.com
Subject: Re: What's good *now*?
Cc:

 Attachment: Four Generations

Alex,

"Selling in the NOW" means making sure you find out exactly who your prospects are. That includes knowing the effects that different generations may have on the sales process.

It's been said that we've experienced more change in the past 50 years than in the previous 500 years. This has left a wake of out-of-date strategies from four distinctive generations whose points of view and opinions must be taken into account.

"Selling in the NOW" is recognizing different generational groups. Learning to understand, test, and then validate any perceptions they might hold will help you relate to them and gain their trust—and ultimately assist them in buying.

I spelled them out in this attachment, "Four Generations."

Dad

Four Generations

1. Mature (traditionalists) - born 1909 to 1945

- Experienced World War II and possibly also WWI
- Strong belief in duty, honor, country
- Lived through the Great Depression
- Hardworking, loyal
- Slow to embrace change
- See technology as having little value
- Financially conservative
- Strong desire to work out issues and meet company goals

Many traditionalists today are approaching retirement or have retired and hold temporary positions in an organization.

2. Baby Boomers - born 1946 to 1964

- Born to post-WWII parents
- Make up 28% of the population and 48% of the workforce
- Raised to believe they can accomplish anything
- Willing to give up family for advancement of career
- Competitively seek advancement because of their numbers
- Seek to please management, thus becoming skilled at company politics
- Look down on others who don't come into the office early and leave late
- Pay attention to the amount of time spent at the office versus what gets accomplished
- Place efforts on acquiring wealth

- *Value learning new things*
- *Rebellious toward existing policy, especially if it's not geared toward their personal goals*

3. Generation Xers – born 1965 to 1984

- *Raised in times of rapid change*
- *Make up approximately 16% of the population*
- *Technologically savvy*
- *Have witnessed major layoffs*
- *Do not expect employer loyalty*
- *Change jobs quickly*
- *Work is not the most important thing in their lives; they seek a balance*
- *Work hard and expect to be well compensated*
- *Favor receiving money today versus future benefits (stock options, vesting bonuses, etc.)*
- *Want to be regarded as individuals rather than be labeled by what they do.*

4. Millennials – born 1981 to 1999

- *Recent college graduates entering the marketplace*
- *Grew up in the computer age*
- *Can apply technology to the workplace easily*
- *Confident and ambitious*
- *Skilled at retrieving volumes of information via the internet*
- *Entrepreneurial and resourceful*
- *Eager to learn and enjoy questioning*
- *Desire career options that are open-ended*
- *Can multitask with ease*
- *Have a sense of civic duty*
- *Their ambition is greater than their knowledge of how to execute new things*

From: Alex@Intecostel.com
To: Rich@RichLucia.com
Subject: Birth certificates
Cc:

Dad,

So all I have to do is request a prospect's birth certificate or a copy of a driver's license before I make a call? LOL!

Alex

From: Rich@RichLucia.com
To: Alex@Intecostel.com
Subject: Once again
Cc:

Alex,

Please don't miss the point with your ready-fire-without aiming sarcasms, son.

These descriptions of the generations are not meant to pigeon-hole anyone. You're not supposed to go out there blindly assuming everyone's personality and habits are an absolute function of the date they were born.

That information is meant to help you understand that generations are different. Many selling tools designed to appeal to a certain time and generation just might not work for the next generation. Get it?

I've given you these generational guidelines (yes, they're just guidelines) so you can be aware of them. You *must* test and validate these generalities through questioning.

And yes, exceptions always exist. I know many Traditionalists who teach computer technology and Baby Boomers who join companies because they want that gold watch at retirement.

Dad

From: Alex@Intecostel.com
To: Rich@RichLucia.com
Subject: I get it
Cc:

Dad,

Sure, I get it. That's why you're sending me emails and not sales text books. LOL!

Alex

From: Rich@RichLucia.com
To: Alex@Intecostel.com
Subject: You broke the code
Cc:

 Attachment: Selling in the NOW

Alex,

You got it. Also, that's why you enjoy questioning me and being sarcastic.

But I have an advantage. I've lived with you and know you have a great deal of Millennial in you. But I also know you've taken in some Baby Boomer influence through osmosis.

My point is this: You can't make assumptions about people. However, having this generational information can give you a jump-start on where to probe when getting to know your prospects.

"Selling in the NOW" means *living in the now*— understanding what goes on around you and how it affects different people. It helps you customize your selling efforts.

Dad

Selling in the NOW

- *Times and people change.*
- *Sales tools designed for one generation might not work for another.*
- *Each generation defines its own motivation factors.*
- *Adjust your selling style and tools to what motivates your prospects.*
- *Understand your prospects' viewpoints.*

There is no selling tool that is "one size fits all" because your prospects are not all one size. Strive to understand your prospects and you will understand their motivations.

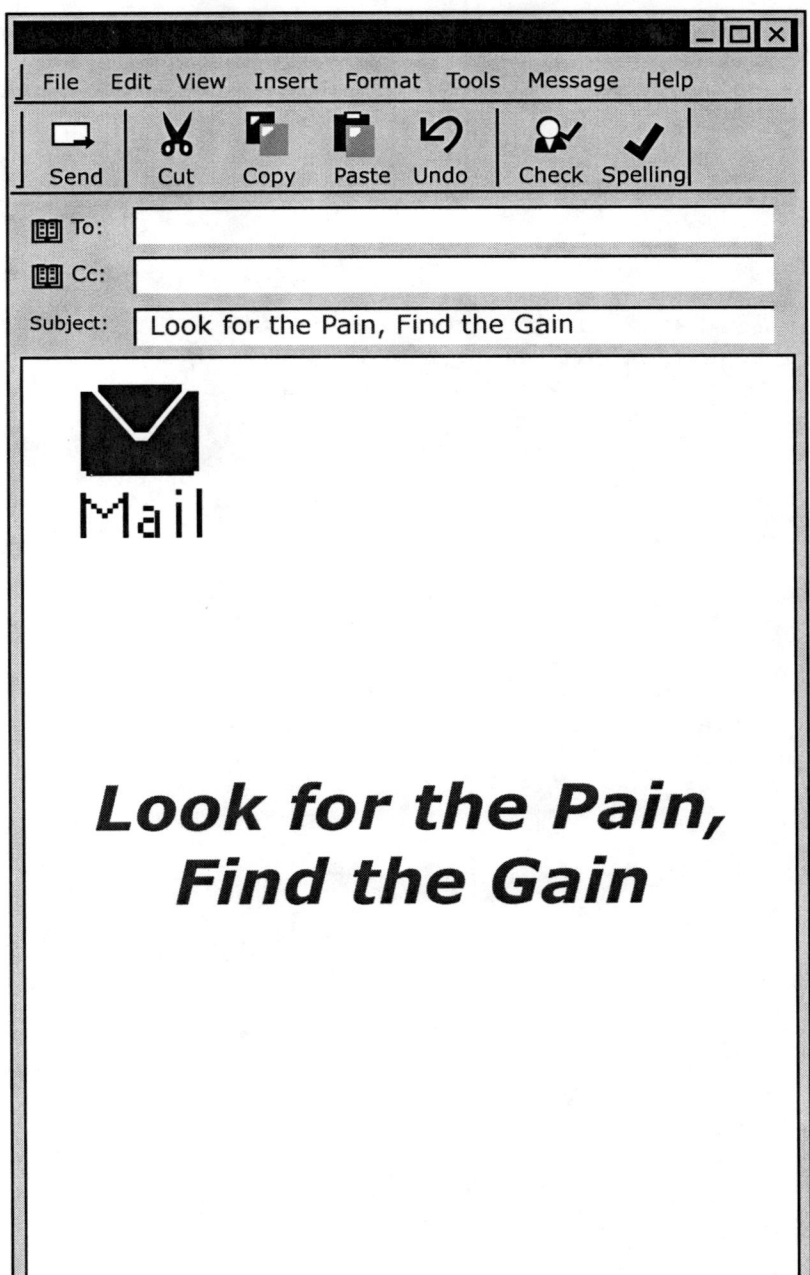

From: Alex@Intecostel.com
To: Rich@RichLucia.com
Subject: Customer motivation
Cc:

Dad,

I understand that different customers have different motivations, but my product is my product regardless. They're either motivated to buy it or not.

Alex

From: Rich@RichLucia.com
To: Alex@Intecostel.com
Subject: Perception
Cc:

Alex,

It's how your customers perceive your product that's important. Of course, if they have no need for it, then there's no sale. But I'm talking about how you *present* your product.

If the way you present its benefits appeals to their pain, they have reason to buy. If it appeals to what's important to them, their gain, that's motivation to buy.

Dad

From: Alex@Intecostel.com
To: Rich@RichLucia.com
Subject: Training sessions here
Cc:

Dad,

It's crazy that during our emails about customers, my company held a questioning training session.

The session covered a lot of sample questions, but the major theme was this: "As you ask your prospects questions, look for their pain in their answers."

I think that means to take time to find out, "What keeps them up at night?" Then zero in on how my product can relieve their pain.

Pretty cool, huh?

Alex

From:	Rich@RichLucia.com
To:	Alex@Intecostel.com
Subject:	Glad to hear you're getting training
Cc:	

Alex,

A lot of sales training today includes the same techniques and tools that were taught years ago. Concepts like "look for the pain" have been taught time and time again.

I'm not saying that just because they've been around, they are no longer valid. But you do have to update these ideas if you want to "Sell in the NOW."

If you don't want to spend your time circling the drain, then you also have to find your customers' gain.

Dad

From: Alex@Intecostel.com
To: Rich@RichLucia.com
Subject: Pain/Gain
Cc:

Dad,

Actually, this pain/gain thing just isn't flushing for me. I don't get it. How do I apply this idea?

Alex

From: Rich@RichLucia.com
To: Alex@Intecostel.com
Subject: Look for the pain; sell to the gain
Cc:

📎 Attachment: Uncover the Pain, Find the Gain

Alex,

Solving pain is a defense play. No one likes pain, but in today's world, it's no longer the only motivator to buy something. Gain is an offense play and a motivator that brings pleasure.

Think of it this way. You won't find people scalping appointments at the dentist's office, but you will find people eagerly scalping tickets at a popular concert. What I'm saying is if you want to move toward assisting your prospect to buy, uncover the two motivations - pain and the gain.

Dad

Uncover the Pain, Find the Gain

It's no longer enough to just read a copy of the company's annual report as part of your due diligence. Unless you're dealing with a corporate officer or members of the board, chances are your prospects haven't read it themselves.

In fact, they generally believe that stated corporate objectives are too far removed from their own department's priorities. Therefore, they relate better to Motivation #2 (for the good of the department) and Motivation #3 (for the good of the individual buyer).

It's possible that someone's motivation can be tagged into more than one category. But, still, you must uncover the pain and find the gain in all three categories before you begin any type of sales presentation.

Motivation #1: Good of the company. This solves a problem that's present in the company or addresses the way things are currently done or not done (e.g., an improvement or process that aligns with corporate goals and objectives).

Motivation #2: Good of the buyer's department or business unit. This addresses a problem that's present in a particular area of a company (e.g., how the department or business unit will be viewed by others politically).

Motivation #3: Good for the individual buyer. This benefits the buyer directly on a personal level. (e.g., less time on the job and more time for personal priorities).

From: Alex@Intecostel.com
To: Rich@RichLucia.com
Subject: Pain/Gain
Cc:

Dad,

So if I'm reading you right, "pain and gain" works this way:

Pain avoids the things that the prospects' personalities tell them they must avoid; gain is what they run toward.

So a Traditionalist might avoid dealing with a proposal or information in an electronic format, yet will willingly accept an idea that shows loyalty to the company and its mission.

Isn't that right?

Alex

From: Rich@RichLucia.com
To: Alex@Intecostel.com
Subject: Got it
Cc:

Alex,

You got it. And Baby Boomers might be attracted to the way your product will make them look good in the eyes of their managers, while a return on investment of ten years won't impress a Generation Xer's personality.

But again, be careful not to assume. Use your questioning skills to validate whatever values each prospect holds. Don't just run and whip out a sales tool just because it's handy.

Dad

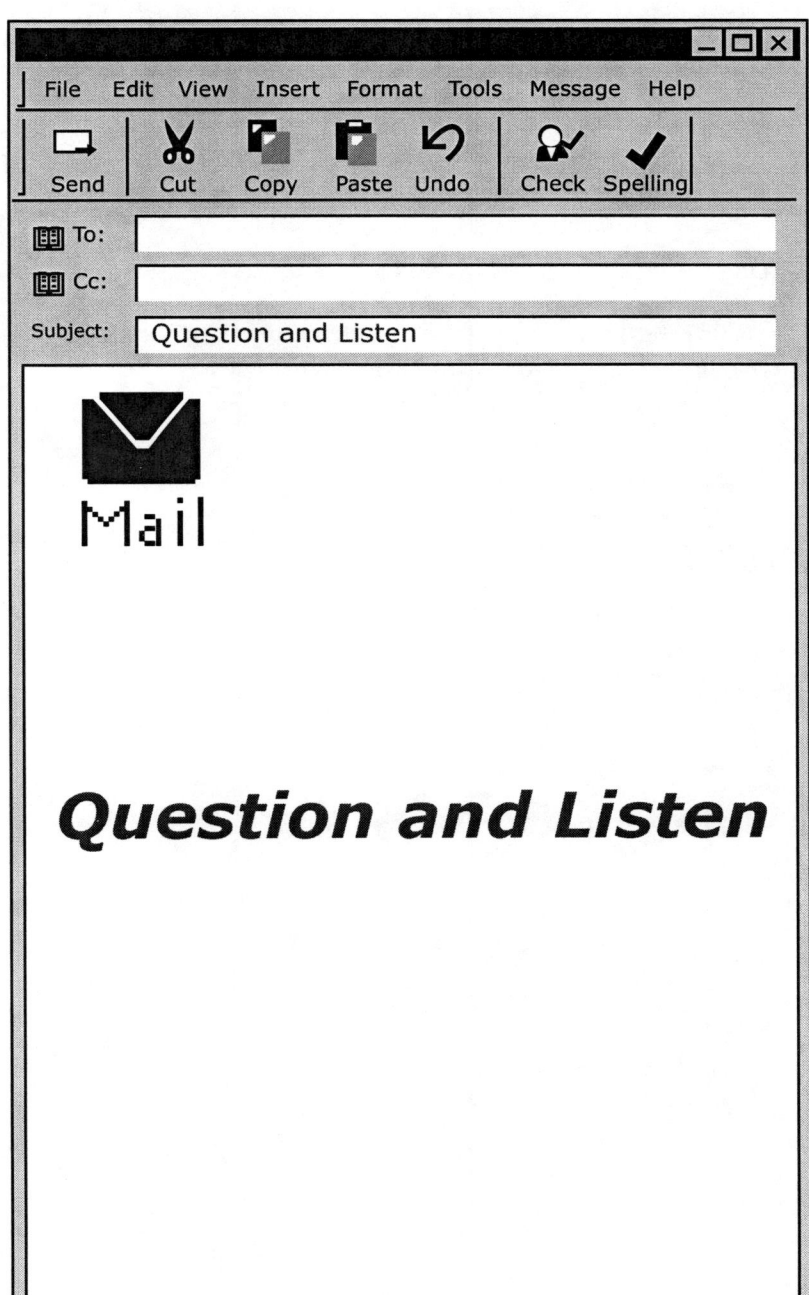

From: Alex@Intecostel.com
To: Rich@RichLucia.com
Subject: That's what they said in sales training
Cc:

Dad,

We learned a lot about this questioning stuff in sales training, but frankly, I forget which questions I'm supposed to ask when I'm with a prospect. I need a script to remember.

Alex

From: Rich@RichLucia.com
To: Alex@Intecostel.com
Subject: Questioning
Cc:

Alex,

You can't memorize words to be spoken in a conversation unless the person you are talking to is also using a script. But that isn't real communication; that's putting on a play for others to enjoy.

Think of all the conversations you've had in which you wanted more information because you were sincerely interested in learning more. Was your part of the conversation scripted? Or did you listen carefully so you could ask further questions?

In a selling situation, it should be the same. But sometimes our training steps in and tries to script the conversations that should come out naturally.

So first and foremost, ask questions to seek information and make the conversation interesting.

Dad

From: Alex@Intecostel.com
To: Rich@RichLucia.com
Subject: Open questions
Cc:

Dad,

We learned about open questions in sales training. You know, the ones for which you can't get one-word answers.

Open questions begin with:
- *Who*
- *Why*
- *What*
- *Where*
- *How*

But even using these kinds of questions, I still feel like I'm grilling my prospect rather than having a natural conversation.

Alex

From: Rich@RichLucia.com
To: Alex@Intecostel.com
Subject: Questioning
Cc:

Alex,

You feel like you're grilling your prospect because *that's exactly what you're doing*.

The purpose of asking questions at this stage is to gain information. Don't let "salesperson training" train the real person out of you. You were hired because someone believes you have the communication skills to interact well with those the company wants to connect with. But when you're regurgitating a list of questions, you're not being yourself. Any prospect can see when you're not being real.

Questions are the tools of dialogue. Each question you ask should be different, specific, and used at the right time. Questions asked skillfully and caringly will not only help you glean the information you seek, but will also build the rapport and respect needed to move forward.

Forget about scripted questions. *Really care.* Be truly interested. You'll learn volumes because you display sincerity and gain their trust.

Dad

From: Alex@Intecostel.com
To: Rich@RichLucia.com
Subject: Thanks for the confidence
Cc:

Dad,

Thanks for the vote of confidence. I will try to be more natural in my approach. It's just that I feel mechanical out there sometimes—always afraid I'll say the wrong thing, or forget to ask or say the right thing.

Alex

From: Rich@RichLucia.com
To: Alex@Intecostel.com
Subject: Natural
Cc:

Alex,

Everyone thrives for natural behavior, and why not? It can be repeated easily without a lot of thought, and, if performed correctly, yields a consistent result. That's why sports champions such as golfers and tennis players strive to develop a natural swing.

When I was growing up and caught a cold, your grandmother told me to drink fluids because they would flush out my system and poof . . . the cold would be gone. Your grandfather, realizing that one could only drink so many fluids before quenching their thirst, said, "Eat saltine crackers." I thought something magical was in a saltine cracker that would cure my cold. But he was going for the natural behavior. He knew that if I ate something salty, I'd be thirsty and drink plenty of fluids.

Be yourself, son, and look for crackers.

Dad

From: Alex@Intecostel.com
To: Rich@RichLucia.com
Subject: Gotta hear this one
Cc:

Dad,

The other day, I made a sales call and tried to follow your direction, but the prospects drove me crazy. They didn't talk about anything close to my product's solution. They just talked and talked and talked about golfing and the problem they were having with the parking lot paving company. What a waste of time.

I tried asking questions that would lead to my product's solution, but one guy just cut me off and said he had another meeting to go to. What's up with that?

Alex

From: Rich@RichLucia.com
To: Alex@Intecostel.com
Subject: It's not about you!
Cc:

Alex,

It seems what you have identified as a problem was an opportunity in disguise. This prospect wanted to talk about what was important to him. What he said gave you an opportunity to use your listening guidelines and gain his respect by showing you care about his problems, whatever they are.

Remember, you are there to gain information and earn the right to gain more information. That doesn't always involve hearing what you *think* you should hear. Let the person talk. When you do, rapport and respect develop naturally.

Your caring about what matters to the other person is the most important thing, not what *you* care about.

Dad

From: Alex@Intecostel.com
To: Rich@RichLucia.com
Subject: Prospect pounce
Cc:

Dad,

Are you saying that I can get rid of that "prospect pounce" thing and build trust by the questions I ask and how I ask them?

Alex

From: Rich@RichLucia.com
To: Alex@Intecostel.com
Subject: Almost, and there's more
Cc:

Alex,

You can only build trust over time. In a first meeting, you can begin to build respect, which will lead to trust—that is, if you always make good on your word and do what you promise.

By asking the right questions and taking time to listen to your prospects' answers—and I mean *really* listen and care about what is said—you'll gain respect and the right to move forward. I don't mean "Bobble Head listening" where you stand there with a stupid grin, your head tilted to the side, and nod over and over again.

Why do you listen? You listen—

- *to gain information*
- *to build respect and rapport*
- *to show empathy and caring*

And then you listen to construct the right questions so you can listen to listen some more.

Dad

From: Alex@Intecostel.com
To: Rich@RichLucia.com
Subject: Listening
Cc:

Dad,

I get the "listening to answer a question" thing, but I'm not sure about this "how to listen" stuff.

Alex

From: Rich@RichLucia.com
To: Alex@Intecostel.com
Subject: Caring and listening
Cc:

 Attachment: Question & Listen

Alex,

Once in a seminar, I talked about great listeners not only learning volumes about their prospects, but about them creating feelings of sincerity, rapport, and respect. After my talk, a salesperson came up to me and asked, "What technique or trick can I use to make customers feel that I care about what they are saying?" I responded with these two words: *"Really Care."*

You see, as a salesperson, you have a great job. You get to meet new people with new ideas and learn things about them, their companies, their products, and their customers.

This is the journey to be enjoyed. That's why I say the money you can earn is a bonus during and at the end of a great experience. You're supposed to enjoy the ride.

Dad

Question & Listen

Ask only the questions you plan on listening to so you can—

- *Gain information*
- *Build respect and rapport*
- *Show empathy and caring*

Listen carefully so you can construct questions that help you do more of all of these.

How do you listen to show you really care?

Really Care!

From: Alex@Intecostel.com
To: Rich@RichLucia.com
Subject: Ready to go
Cc:

Dad,

Just finished putting together all my stuff. I've got my car organized with business cards, brochures, and a pitch book. My manager says to just jump right in and don't be afraid of making a mistake. But if I make mistakes, I won't make any sales. Can you help me please?

Alex

From: Rich@RichLucia.com
To: Alex@Intecostel.com
Subject: Make a list
Cc:

Alex,

Your manager is right. Don't be afraid of making mistakes. But still, know that you can find ways to help maximize your efforts while cutting your losses.

You'll *always* find yourself with a new product or service to sell. So take time to plan where you want to go with your questioning and presentation, and in what order.

First, make a list of prospects that would receive the most benefit from your offering and rank them, in list format, from the most valuable to the least valuable. Then turn the list upside down and start making calls. You won't be at your best on the phone until you get about half way through the list. This way, when you get to the best opportunities, you will have practiced and perfected your skills.

Good luck,

Dad

From: Alex@Intecostel.com
To: Rich@RichLucia.com
Subject: Where are they?
Cc:

Dad,

I hear your advice, Dad, but where do I *find* prospects who really want to buy from me?

Alex

From: Rich@RichLucia.com
To: Alex@Intecostel.com
Subject: Customer Profile
Cc:

 Attachment: Prospecting

Alex,

Follow these steps first:

1. Develop in your mind the ideal customers for your product.
2. Make a list of why they would need your product.
3. Determine where these "ideal customers" reside.
4. Make an action plan to contact and visit as many of them as you can.
5. Develop a list of questions to ask these prospects and learn about their needs.

We are aiming here, no firing yet. Leave the pitch book behind.

Dad

Prospecting

- *Make a list of target customers.*
- *Prioritize them from most valuable to least.*
- *Flip the list over and start making calls.*

The best information about why someone should buy your product isn't in any brochure or website; it comes out of the mouth of existing customers.

From: Alex@Intecostel.com
To: Rich@RichLucia.com
Subject: I got my list
Cc:

Dad,

No offense, but some of the people on my "Ideal Customer Profile" list were people I'd already made my pitch to. And they weren't buying.

Alex

From: Rich@RichLucia.com
To: Alex@Intecostel.com
Subject: You were pitching instead of catching
Cc:

Alex,

That's my point. You walked in *pitching* and not *listening*.

You have to first find out what's most important to your prospects. Remember earlier when I explained that being a salesperson is helping find a solution to a problem? How can you accomplish that without fully understanding what the potential customer perceives as a need or problem? You can't assume, you have to *know*. You gain that information by asking questions.

Dad

From: Alex@Intecostel.com
To: Rich@RichLucia.com
Subject: Blank stares
Cc:

Dad,

I'm starting to feel pretty comfortable about my product knowledge. I have all the features and benefits memorized and even won a demo contest at our last sales meeting. But I'm still getting blank stares and being cut short when I do my presentation. Got any thoughts?

Alex

From: Rich@RichLucia.com
To: Alex@Intecostel.com
Subject: Questions for existing customers
Cc:

Alex,

By now, you've learned how to gain the information you need to relate. However, prospects don't like to be loners. They want to know that other companies have purchased your product.

Some salespeople think they can satisfy this need with a page of logos from customer companies. But doing that only satisfies the "I'm not first" fear. You need real, live stories about known, satisfied clients to tell your prospects.

So ask your manager if you can visit some existing customers with the sales representative in that territory or with the manager. When you get there, ask these customers about using your company's product, and how that helped them. What did they use before your company's solution? What made them buy?

Yes, you got it. You're uncovering what was their *pain* and learning about their *gain*.

Dad

From:	Alex@Intecostel.com
To:	Rich@RichLucia.com
Subject:	Existing customers
Cc:	

Dad,

That might be tough. Most salespeople are very protective of their customers and a lot of the existing customers are handled by a different sales manager than I have. But I'll find out and give this idea a try.

Alex

From: Rich@RichLucia.com
To: Alex@Intecostel.com
Subject: Don't check your guns at the door
Cc:

Alex,

In the old west, bar owners would require that cowboys leave their guns on a hook at the door. They didn't want drunken arguments turning into destructive gunfights on their premises. Selling isn't for just "out there"; use your sales ability in your own company. Don't check your guns at the door when you walk through your company's door. Convince the sales managers that you can leverage more sales with the knowledge you'll gain from people in the company.

Let's apply the "180 Rule." If your company didn't want to leverage its existing sales success, what would the managers do?

Dad

From: Alex@Intecostel.com
To: Rich@RichLucia.com
Subject: Customer testimonials
Cc:

Dad,

The "180 Rule" says that we'd only give out names of our existing customers when asked.

Hey, we have a few glossy handouts featuring customer testimonials. Maybe I can just use those.

Alex

From: Rich@RichLucia.com
To: Alex@Intecostel.com
Subject: You're copping out
Cc:

Alex,

What's important to your sales managers?
Sales, right?

If you can deliver on your idea of customer visits and close more sales, they will love you. Customers and opportunities don't have territories; only sales teams do. Work the way customers think, not the way you're organized. Prospects love to hear what is going on across the street, especially in their industry and specifically with their competition. They also love to hear how people in their positions get their jobs done. So get out there and share information.

Try this. Ask a few salespeople in your company about their customers. Use the same questions I sent you earlier for the customers themselves. I'll bet you'll get answers like, "They use this model," but little more. What's that all about? If you don't know the answer to those questions, it means you don't know your current customers. How can you relate to a new one?

Dad

From: Alex@Intecostel.com
To: Rich@RichLucia.com
Subject: It worked!
Cc:

Dad,

Thanks. It appears that the power of questioning and listening is paying off. I got to talk to several existing customers. Also, my prospects seem to want to talk to me more and I'm getting more comfortable interacting with them. You were right; they really do like to hear about people in the same boat as they are.

Now I'm eager to land some sales. But I guess I just have to live with my product's order cycle before I get to see results.

Alex

From: Rich@RichLucia.com
To: Alex@Intecostel.com
Subject: You're welcome
Cc:

Alex,

About your product's order cycle, I'm assuming you mean the length of time it takes from the first contact until you secure an order.

If so, how would you describe the order cycle in your company?

Dad

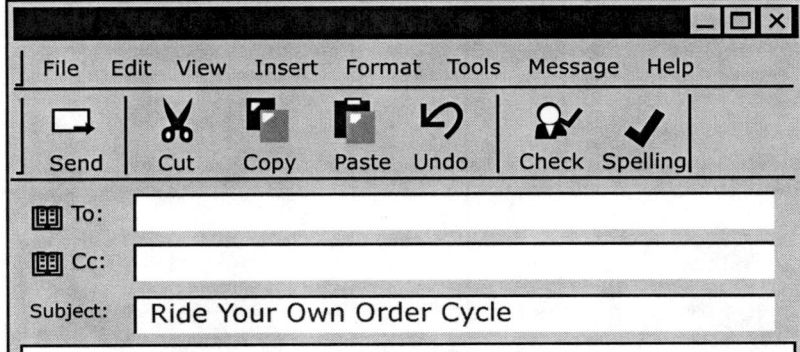

From: Alex@Intecostel.com
To: Rich@RichLucia.com
Subject: Order cycle
Cc:

Dad,

Yes, our company's order cycle, from the time of contacting a prospect to the completion of an initial sale, is about seven to eight months. It's long. That's why my manager wants to see a full pipeline of prospects.

I'm also concerned with the holidays coming up and dwindling sales that happen this time of year. People are busy and traveling.

Alex

From: Rich@RichLucia.com
To: Alex@Intecostel.com
Subject: Order Cycle
Cc:

Alex,

Your manager is right about keeping a full pipeline. However, the whole idea of a set order cycle is nonsense. And needing a season for selling is also an excuse that salespeople make.

I once worked for three companies all in the same technology space. Each one of them did 60% to 65% of their total year's sales in the last two months of their fiscal year. Hear is the best part:

One had a fiscal year ending in December.
One had a fiscal year ending in June.
One had a fiscal year ending in March.

The difference wasn't the month of the year, but the motivation of the sales force!

You, too, can have a positive effect on your order cycle by the actions you take.

Dad

From: Alex@Intecostel.com
To: Rich@RichLucia.com
Subject: You got my attention
Cc:

Dad,

If you have some magical way to get my prospects to buy more quickly, I'm in. I would like to not only "Sell in the NOW" but "Get the order NOW."

Alex

From: Rich@RichLucia.com
To: Alex@Intecostel.com
Subject: Moving the cycle
Cc:

Alex,

There's nothing magical about it. If it's seven to eight months from the first contact with a prospect, it's because you're taking them through the sales funnel, starting from the top. What if you could bring a prospect into the funnel further along in the sale's cycle?

Growers have to pick tomatoes when they're green because they need a certain number of days to ripen and get to the store. Prospects don't have to work the same way.

If you have the opportunity, pick a ripe one now. Find prospects that are already in the sales process with your competitor. Maybe you'll get lucky and talk with them as they're about to place an order. You may find they've taken the time to get clear about what they want and why. Even if they're entrenched in your competitor's sales cycle, you can address their pain/gain—and perhaps change their decision in your favor.

Dad

From: Alex@Intecostel.com
To: Rich@RichLucia.com
Subject: Can that be done?
Cc:

Dad,

Can you really take a sale away from someone late in the sales cycle?

Alex

From: Rich@RichLucia.com
To: Alex@Intecostel.com
Subject: Absolutely
Cc:

Alex,

It's done every day. As a matter of fact, when you apply "Selling in the NOW," prospects get to a point in the sales cycle when they want to make a quick decision. Catch them then—after everyone else has done the heavy lifting. Not only will you get the sale, but you'll be thanked for adding clarity to the situation.

Remember, the most exciting part of a football game is the last ten minutes.

Dad

From: Alex@Intecostel.com
To: Rich@RichLucia.com
Subject: How do you get there?
Cc:

Dad,

How do you get in the game late? What can I do to find out who's on my competitors' forecast list?

Alex

From: Rich@RichLucia.com
To: Alex@Intecostel.com
Subject: Change your viewpoint
Cc:

 Attachment: Order Cycle

Alex,

You can find who is currently in a buy cycle by adjusting your PA (that's your Prospecting Attitude).

That means changing from looking for prospects who *might* have a need to prospects *already in the buy cycle*.

Here's how:

- *Go to trade shows and ask outright, "Are you in the process of looking at a _____?" (name your solution)*
- *Call someone in the decision maker's department (but not the decision maker) and ask if the company is looking for a product like yours. If not, move on.*
- *Check with salespeople in other companies who deal in the same space as you do, but not the same product as yours. Ask what is going on in their account.*
- *Sometimes when you talk with an in-cycle prospect and ask who else (among your competitors) is being considered, he or she knows from talking with a chatty competitor.*

Be creative. You'll be surprised how you can shorten your sales cycle by focusing on in-cycle prospects.

Dad

Order Cycle

- *In many cases, the order cycle is determined by your activity.*
- *Get into the sales cycle at the end.*
- *Focus on hunting for ready-now buying prospects.*

Did you ever notice that when you're ready to buy something (like a particular make of car), you see hundreds of them on the road and can easily describe the model and features of each? Catch your prospects in that mindset and their hearts will follow.

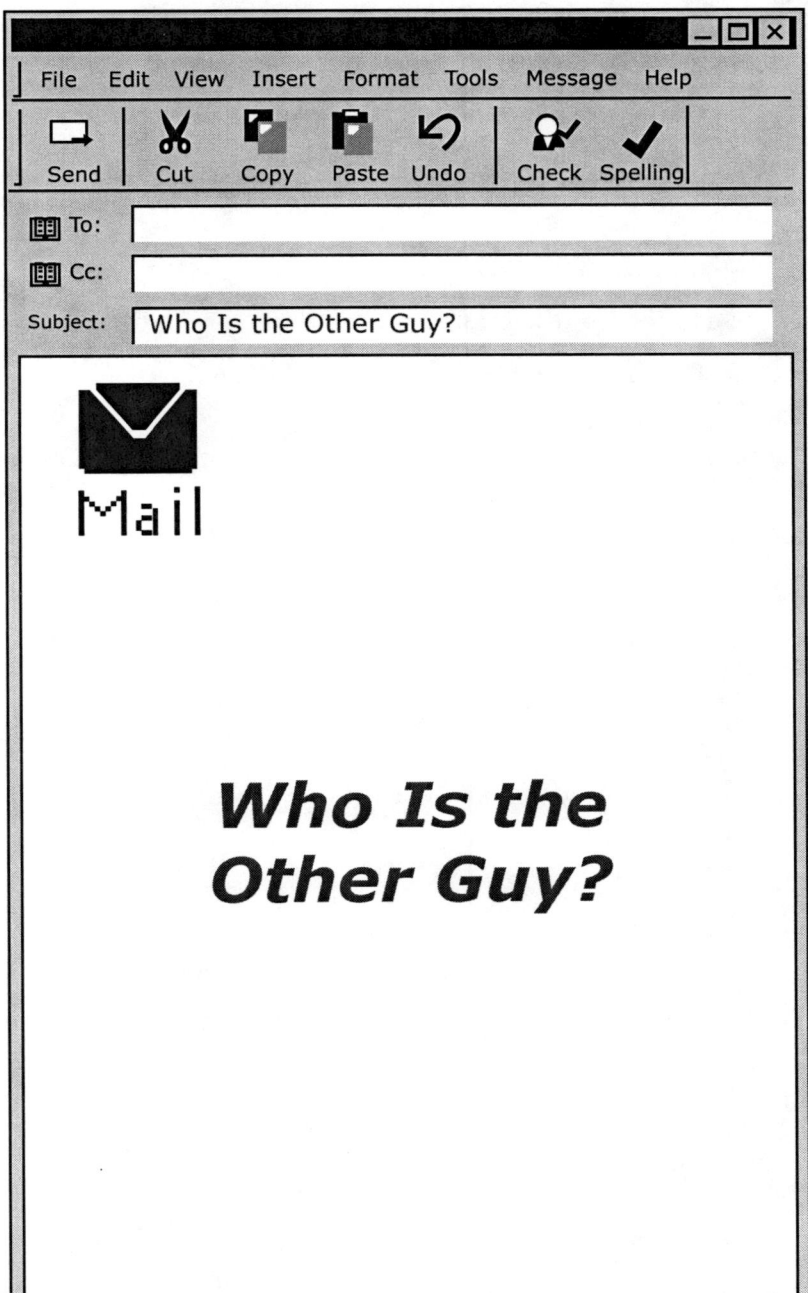

From: Alex@Intecostel.com
To: Rich@RichLucia.com
Subject: I can beat those bums
Cc:

Dad,

We just had a great sales meeting on competition. I got some wonderful zingers to hit my prospects with in the future. Our competitors don't have a chance. I can bury them.

Alex

From: Rich@RichLucia.com
To: Alex@Intecostel.com
Subject: How to treat the competition
Cc:

Alex,

It's always great to learn new things about dealing with competitors. However, think twice before you run out there and knock anyone or anything. It might be viewed as pushy and manipulative. Stay on the high ground. Never knock your competition. Instead, praise them. That's right—**praise them**.

If you did a decent job of uncovering your prospects' pain and finding their gain, you'll know what they favor and what they don't. The idea is to praise your competitors on everything they do that's *not* of interest to your prospects.

Again, use the "180 Rule." What features do your customers place no value in? Which ones do they dislike? Point out that these are the things your competition does really well; in fact, they are noted for them. Try it out!

Dad

From: Alex@Intecostel.com
To: Rich@RichLucia.com
Subject: *Praise* them?
Cc:

Dad,

Are you losing it? My competition is my *enemy*. Why in the world would I say anything nice about them? I'm not going to help them make a sale that should be mine!

Alex

From: Rich@RichLucia.com
To: Alex@Intecostel.com
Subject: Praise them out of the sale
Cc:

Alex,

Most sales are lost because the salespeople insist on telling a prospect what *they* think it important, not reinforcing what the *prospect* thinks is important. This goes on until the prospect gets bored and says, "This isn't for me" or until a feature is stressed that the prospect doesn't like.

If you know how to employ the pain/gain concept well, you can accomplish the same thing for your competition and never come across as pushy or malicious. Here's an example: A man wanted to buy a car for his family of four. His two top priorities were safety and comfort. You can praise your competitor's car as being a great sports car that can go from zero to sixty miles per hour in six seconds. A statement like that certainly won't get your prospect to lean toward buying from your competitor.

Stay on the high ground. Both you and your customer get a better view from there.

Dad

From: Alex@Intecostel.com
To: Rich@RichLucia.com
Subject: The other guy
Cc:

Dad,

My manager says it's best to get the "competition thing" on the table right at the beginning. We're told to talk about all the other competitors with our prospects and get everything out in the open. I even have a handout that points out all our competitors and their shortfalls compared with my company.

Alex

From: Rich@RichLucia.com
To: Alex@Intecostel.com
Subject: How you pick your battles
Cc:

Alex,

I admire your manager's sense of "going right to war," but it's up to *you* to pick the battle and the best time to do so. Ask this question: Would you ever want to make your prospects aware of your competition's existence?

Competitive information is knowledge you use as background, not something you volunteer to prospects. Why bring more players into *your* game?

I get the biggest kick out of how salespeople get free tickets from a trade show promoter and pass them out to their customers. Generally, these tickets come with a proud "come see me at the show." But they are *your* customers. You can see them anytime. Why use the tickets to bring them to a venue where your competitors hang out?

Let's use the "180 Rule." Where would you invite your customers if you wanted them to see your competitors?

What kind of handouts would you create if you wanted to bring in your competitors? Leave the free tickets at home.

Dad

From: Alex@Intecostel.com
To: Rich@RichLucia.com
Subject: Competition
Cc:

Dad,

Some customers need to hear about all competitors because they have to submit a report comparing their differences.

Alex

From: Rich@RichLucia.com
To: Alex@Intecostel.com
Subject: Competition
Cc:

Alex,

Hold that thought about your prospect having to write up a report. That might be a red flag that you're not dealing with the decision maker. But we will leave that be for now. I'm talking about introducing new competition to your prospect.

For a time, I was that decision maker that salespeople pitched to. One time, a salesperson began telling me how their features were so much better than ABC Company and XYZ Company. I didn't even *know* ABC Company and XYZ Company were in the business, let alone what features they offered.

As a matter of fact, XYZ Company sounded interesting, so I looked into their offering. Beyond the turn off of the salesperson being nonprofessional by knocking someone else, I had a new reason to not go forward. Armed with new competitive information, I wanted to look some more.

Dad

From: Alex@Intecostel.com
To: Rich@RichLucia.com
Subject: Uhhhhhh
Cc:

Dad,

That was ugly! I never want to set that up!

Alex

From: Rich@RichLucia.com
To: Alex@Intecostel.com
Subject: Competition – more thoughts
Cc:

 Attachment: Competition

Alex,

A final word on competition. Your true competition is not another company with a similar product or service. It's actually *everyone* with whom your prospect has come in contact.

One day, I went to the dry cleaner and was greeted with, "Hello, Mr. Lucia. Here are your shirts. We noticed that there was a button missing so we replaced it. Have a great day." I said thank you and went on to my bank where I waited in line. The teller ignored me as he lined up all the faces on a stack of U.S. Bills. (It's not like the presidents could see anyway.) Now, I haven't been in contact with a competitive bank for years, but who do you think I was comparing my bank to? You got it - the dry cleaner.

The next day—without any encouragement from another bank—I changed where I bank so I could get better customer service.

I say, "Aim to be the most professional, most sincere person your prospect ever met—not just the best in your industry."

Dad

P.S. I've attached a message for you on competition.

Competiton

- *Use pain/gain information.*
- *Know competitive features.*
- *Praise competition on features that have little or no interest to your prospects.*

Never volunteer a competitor's name and never knock any company. Stay on the high road. Be the best professional your prospect ever met.

From: Alex@Intecostel.com
To: Rich@RichLucia.com
Subject: PowerPoint
Cc:

Dad,

I put together the greatest presentation in PowerPoint. It really drives home the benefits of my company and our products. It's great because it's in electronic format so I can email it to my prospects if I can't get out there to see them personally.

I'll email you a copy and maybe you'll have suggestions on what to add.

Alex

From: Rich@RichLucia.com
To: Alex@Intecostel.com
Subject: Your electronic presentation
Cc:

Alex,

Hold on, Mr. PowerPoint. You just spent a great deal of effort finding out about your prospects—their likes, dislikes, pain, and gain. You listened and learned exactly what will make them buy. You never want to bore them with a one-size-fits-all presentation.

Let me guess. Your PowerPoint starts with the history of your company, then a standard problem that your product addresses, followed by a detailed description of your product, a page full of installed customer logos, and finally a single blank page with the word "questions" at the top. Right?

Dad

From: Alex@Intecostel.com
To: Rich@RichLucia.com
Subject: A unique presentation for each one?
Cc:

Dad,

That's pretty much it. Plus some diagrams showing how the product works.

Are you saying that I have to create a unique presentation for every prospect I present to?

Alex

From: Rich@RichLucia.com
To: Alex@Intecostel.com
Subject: Why not?
Cc:

Alex,

The best you'll ever get by giving the same presentation to everyone is a hope that something in it appeals to someone. Save the one-size-fits-all presentation for when you're giving an overview to a group of 100 prospects. Then you have no choice except to throw your line in the crowd and hope someone bites on it.

When presenting to an individual prospect, the material should be about solving that person's problems. Focus on pain and gain, not a history of how your company started in a garage and is now worth a zillion dollars. If you gathered your information properly, you'll know what they care about.

Again, use the "180 Rule." How would you treat your prospects if you wanted to make them feel like the time and information they shared with you was being ignored?

Dad

From: Alex@Intecostel.com
To: Rich@RichLucia.com
Subject: That's a lot of work!
Cc:

Dad,

Does everyone really need a custom presentation? That's a lot of work. I'm sure that some prospects want to only get an overview. Right?

Alex

From: Rich@RichLucia.com
To: Alex@Intecostel.com
Subject: Only if you want to close the sale
Cc:

Alex,

That's true if you can't be bothered closing the sale.

Son, what we're talking about is truly understanding what would make your prospect buy. Do you believe you are selling something that doesn't need your personal attention to relate how that product satisfies your prospect's needs? If so, then just place it on e-Bay and call it a day.

As far as it being a lot of work, well it is. Selling is a profession. That's why I want you to understand the things you need to do *every day* and love what you do.

You'll never be at the top of your game or the top of any profession without a passion for what you're doing.

Dad

From: Alex@Intecostel.com
To: Rich@RichLucia.com
Subject: OK, you made your point
Cc:

Dad,

Ok. But how can I be sure I'm presenting what the prospect wants to hear?

Alex

From: Rich@RichLucia.com
To: Alex@Intecostel.com
Subject: Remember what you've already learned
Cc:

 Attachment: The Presentation

Alex,

If you did your questioning and listening correctly, you've got it.

Never guess and never assume. Organize your information and begin by writing an outline for your presentation to your prospect. Then as you prepare it, ask this key question: Does the point on this page benefit this prospect or is it just filler?

By all means, use company-provided support material. But only after it passes the "Is this best for this prospect?" test. If it does, use it. If it *almost* does, modify it. If it doesn't *at all*, leave it out.

Remember what we said as you were growing up in Philly? If it looks good, smell it. If it smells good, eat it.

Dad

The Presentation

- *Don't present assumed information.*

- *Organize your information as it relates to each prospect.*

- *Customize it to address your prospect's pain/gain.*

- *Put the history of the company in a handout, not on the PowerPoint.*

You can't effectively be heard unless you're presenting what someone is willing to hear.

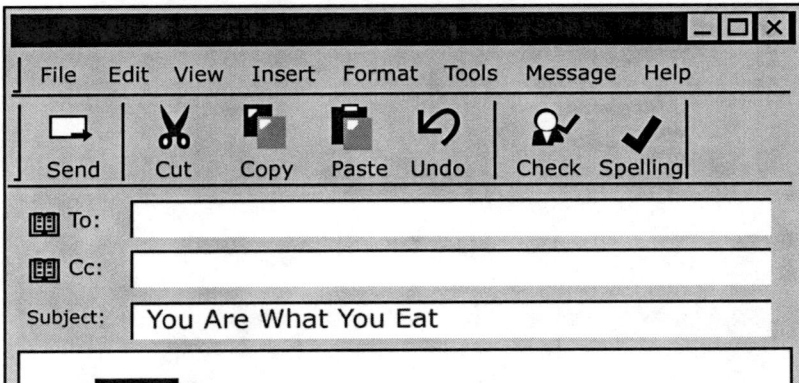

From: Alex@Intecostel.com
To: Rich@RichLucia.com
Subject: This place sucks
Cc:

Dad,

Things are starting to turn around and a lot of what you said has really helped. But I've gotta tell you, this place *sucks*.

I've been hanging out, having a few beers with a couple of other reps I work with, and they all say the same thing. Our compensation plan sucks and the support we get from the company sucks. We are using old laptops and our cell phones are vintage from last year.

Honestly, I don't know if this is the right place for me. We all talk about it a lot, but quitting might be the best thing.

Alex

From: Rich@RichLucia.com
To: Alex@Intecostel.com
Subject: Sorry to hear you're having a tough time
Cc:

Alex,

Do you know the sound a toilet makes when you just push on the handle a little? It's not quite a flush, but the sound of the water beginning to rush tells you that a flush is coming.

That's what I am hearing from you now. It's not quite a flush, but if you don't back off, it will definitely happen. You're on a path that you think you want to take, but before you do, stop a minute and understand how you got there.

You are what you eat. If you take in a constant diet of negative thoughts, you will become negative. It appears you have yourself hooked up with several toxic people. They will bring you down. For many, bringing you down makes them feel above you. That's probably the only way they can achieve what they think is a success.

Think twice before you swallow a lot of negative "beer talk." It's heavy. And like beer, it will weigh you down and go right to your gut.

Dad

From: Alex@Intecostel.com
To: Rich@RichLucia.com
Subject: Picking my friends
Cc:

Dad,

These are my *friends*.

There you go again, trying to tell me who to pick as my friends. You don't understand; we all feel the same way. It's really bad around here. We talk about it every day after work.

Alex

From: Rich@RichLucia.com
To: Alex@Intecostel.com
Subject: Are they really friends?
Cc:

Alex,

You can choose to be with anyone you want, except you need to know that being with the wrong people might just support a wrong outcome.

You say you want to earn in the upper two percent of the population. If you truly want to do that, then you have to do something different than ninety-eight percent of the population. Following any crowd makes you part of the masses. And following losers gets you to the bottom of the food chain.

I do have a question. If the situation sucks so badly, why haven't these friends left the company by now? You know there's only one thing worse than getting upset, *quitting* and *leaving*. That's getting upset, *quitting* and *staying*.

When that happens, you lose, the company loses, and everyone goes home feeling miserable.

Alex, wake up. These people aren't your friends. Friends support your goals; they don't hang out on the dark side. Bring a positive force to your side. Make the force be with you in your current situation.

Dad

From: Alex@Intecostel.com
To: Rich@RichLucia.com
Subject: Good guys
Cc:

Dad,

Let me set you straight right now.

These guys are experienced and have been around this place and this industry for a while. One of them has sold for three other companies before coming here. They know a bad deal when they see it.

I've been looking on Monster.com and see a lot of sales jobs out there that have a bigger base salary than I have now. I'm going to throw my resume out there.

I'll let you know what happens.

Alex

From:	Rich@RichLucia.com
To:	Alex@Intecostel.com
Subject:	I can tell you what will happen
Cc:	

Alex,

Okay. You will find another job, possibly for a bigger base salary. And six months from now, you'll be making that same toilet-half-flush sound. Watch. The process will start all over again.

One of the best features of being in sales is that you're truly in control of your destiny. You can choose how and when you do your job. If you want to make more money, you have the opportunity to do that, too. It's not as though you are in a routine job with a fixed salary until a set time on a calendar. You don't have to wait for a name to fall off an organizational chart before being recognized with a promotion.

Think seriously about what you're doing. Just the act of looking for a new job takes you out of the game. Make sure you really want a new game, and that you're not just looking for an excuse to take a break.

Dad

From: Alex@Intecostel.com
To: Rich@RichLucia.com
Subject: Stay miserable?
Cc:

Dad,

What should I do if I'm not happy? Stay miserable?

Alex

From: Rich@RichLucia.com
To: Alex@Intecostel.com
Subject: Your choice
Cc:

Alex,

No, son, you never have to continue to feel miserable. You always have the power and the opportunity to change your perspective, whether you stay in this job or leave it.

If you're looking to be happy, then let's work on how to get happier—not run into a new situation with no guarantees that it won't come with a new set of problems.

Try this. Miss a week's worth of beer bitch sessions and avoid daytime hallway static with your buddies. Go out and follow what we've been talking about over the past months and close one sale.

Disconnect yourself from toxic people and avoid even looking at Monster.com. (That means no "just-in-case" diffusion of your energy.)

Instead, seek the most successful, positive-minded people in your office and engage in uplifting conversations. Then, if you feel the same way, let's talk.

Promise me you'll give this a try.

Dad

From: Alex@Intecostel.com
To: Rich@RichLucia.com
Subject: OK—no more diffusion
Cc:

Dad,

I'll give it a try. Maybe that diet of whines and complaints was only getting me good at complaining. You know, Dad, I was also feeling tired a lot. I guess this noise really is bogus energy.

Alex

From: Rich@RichLucia.com
To: Alex@Intecostel.com
Subject: Way to go
Cc:

 Attachment: Attitude

Alex,

I'm proud of you. You are about to take a step toward understanding you have the power to control your future and control your life.

Cool!

Dad

P.S. Here's another message on attitude to help you reinforce this resolve.

Attitude

- *You are what you eat. A toxic diet makes you a toxic personality.*

- *Seek positive people to hang out with.*

- *Keep your head in the game—always.*

- *You have the power to change whatever bothers you.*

There is only one thing worse than getting upset, quitting and leaving. It's getting upset, quitting and staying.

From: Alex@Intecostel.com
To: Rich@RichLucia.com
Subject: Closed a big one
Cc:

Dad,

I closed a huge sale today. I feel on top of the world.

It was nip-and-tuck. This prospect was leaning toward another company. But I turned the conversation around and struck gold.

This puts me ahead of my year-to-date quota. It also made me salesperson of the month. Another one this size gets me a monster bonus.

I'm jazzed. I'll let you know how it goes.

Alex

From: Rich@RichLucia.com
To: Alex@Intecostel.com
Subject: Congratulations
Cc:

Alex,

Way to go, killer. Remember the feeling you have right now. Let it drive you to be all you can be. Just like the Hokey Pokey; that's what it's all about.

Dad

From: Alex@Intecostel.com
To: Rich@RichLucia.com
Subject: Thanks, Dad
Cc:

Dad,

It sure feels a whole lot better winning than losing. I appreciate the support you've given me. Hope we can keep it up.

Alex

From: Rich@RichLucia.com
To: Alex@Intecostel.com
Subject: My pleasure
Cc:

Alex,

Keep up the learning, son. Make it a point to work at your profession. Read sales books and articles. Learn more about your customers' businesses. Try to see exactly what they see.

Start by going to your customers' trade shows. Learn about *their* products and *their* customers. Visit with their Sales VP. Offer to keep a lookout for opportunities for their company. Sales executives can be great allies for you if they know the company organization and have empathy for a fellow salesperson.

Use some of your TV time as a way to grow. When you watch TV, you're learning how to buy. When you read sales information, you're learning how to sell. Both are needed.

Dad

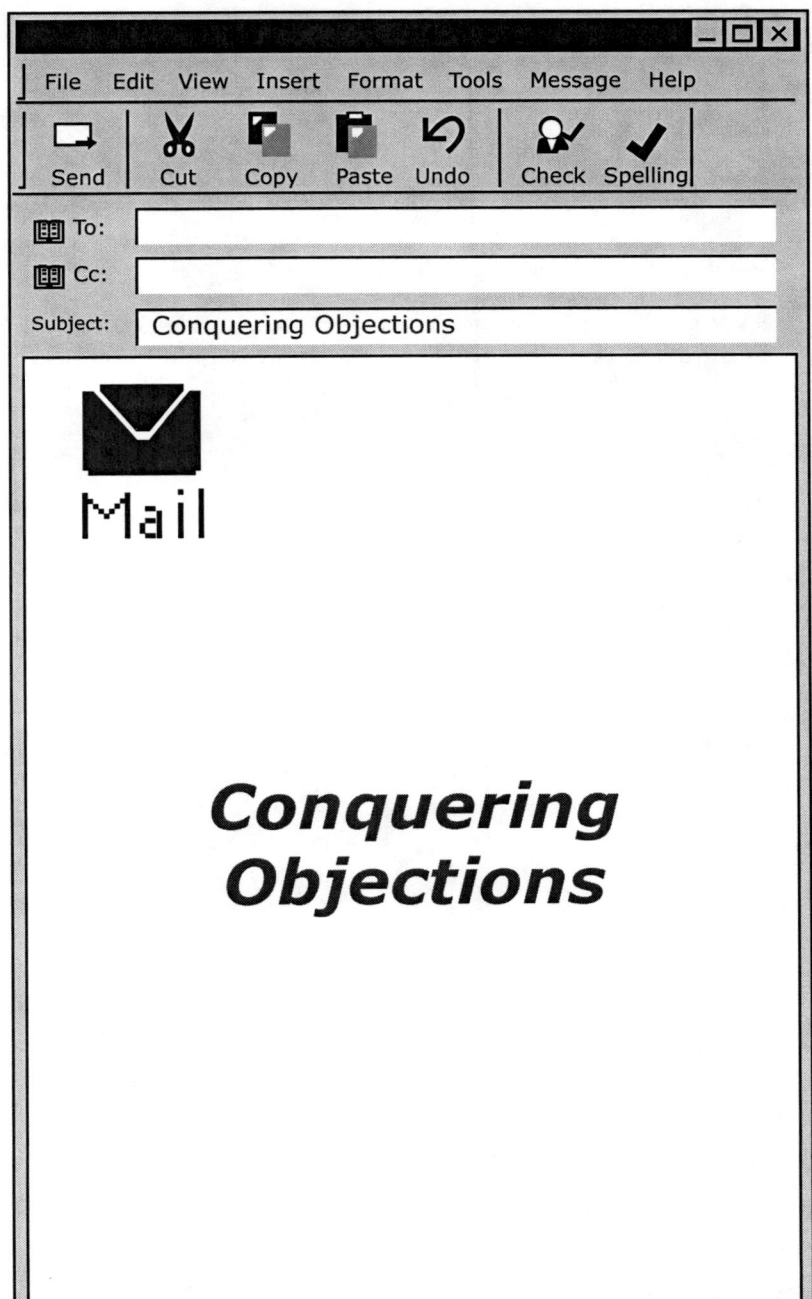

From: Alex@Intecostel.com
To: Rich@RichLucia.com
Subject: It's a jungle out there
Cc:

Dad,

I keep following you advice after all these weeks of emailing. But I seem to be getting a whole lot of objections from prospects these days. They don't need my product . . . they don't have any money . . . they already have something else. Blah blah blah.

What's up?

Alex

From: Rich@RichLucia.com
To: Alex@Intecostel.com
Subject: Swollen
Cc:

Alex,

I worked with a salesman once who was, well, let's say he was a little overweight. No, let's just say he was a *lot* overweight.

But he'd always swear that he wasn't overweight; he was really a skinny guy swollen from being beat up so much by his customers.

Dad

From: Alex@Intecostel.com
To: Rich@RichLucia.com
Subject: Know the feeling
Cc:

Dad,

Some days I feel like everyone I talk to has some sort of objection to what I say. We had a training class on handling objections and some of the reps are really good at quick comebacks. I didn't do too badly myself in the class. But when I got face to face with a prospect, I forgot the canned comebacks we'd learned.

Alex

From: Rich@RichLucia.com
To: Alex@Intecostel.com
Subject: Handling Objections
Cc:

Alex,

Handling objections is a messy process. If you want to avoid getting hit, then avoid the punch. That means "handle" as few objections as possible. They could be real or not, but one thing is for sure—they take time away from the people who really need your product.

Instead, think about "conquering the objection."

Notice I said "conquering the objection" and not "handling" it. As salespeople, we handle objections every day; but when we do, sometimes we win and sometimes we lose. However, when we can *avoid* an objection, we don't waste time and we can't lose.

Dad

From: Alex@Intecostel.com
To: Rich@RichLucia.com
Subject: Run away?
Cc:

Dad,

What? You want me to *run away* from objections?

Alex

From: Rich@RichLucia.com
To: Alex@Intecostel.com
Subject: Objection traps
Cc:

Alex,

Let me clarify. We can agree that our best chance of making that sale is to conquer prospects' objections. For now, we're on a mission to avoid unnecessary objections by hunting for where the business *is* rather than talking to anyone who has a pulse.

We have to take a close look at our product and clearly pinpoint what problem it solves for people. Who is most likely to benefit from using our product or service? What are they using now for solutions? What type of results are they realizing from their current solution? What will be the benefits derived from using a product or service that you can offer? Clearly know who has both the need *and* the motivation to buy your product.

It sounds trite, but if someone doesn't have the motivation to buy your product, then pull out what will now become your first valuable tool in conquering objections: NEXT DOOR. Yes, simply go next door where someone truly has a need. That's where you belong. Do this and you leave behind a whole world of frustration. That's what I mean by avoiding objections.

Dad

From: Alex@Intecostel.com
To: Rich@RichLucia.com
Subject: Avoiding objections
Cc:

Dad,

I never know when objections will come up. Naturally I don't want them; they just come at me. So how do I avoid them?

Alex

From: Rich@RichLucia.com
To: Alex@Intecostel.com
Subject: Conquering
Cc:

Alex,

It takes an understanding of where your prospect's negative feeling originates. I know this flies in the face of all the clever "spin men," who insist on giving you canned responses fresh out of the bag of "When they say this, you say that." But clever is for TV sitcoms, not for satisfying customers' needs.

Closing the gate after the horse leaves the barn makes sense for the future. Chasing and maybe catching the horse handles the problem now. But fixing the lock on the gate in the first place makes the most sense to me.

Conquering objections is about taking steps to keep the lock in place. It's what keeps chasing and handling the horse to a minimum.

Remember all those prospecting ideas we discussed?

Dad

From:	Alex@Intecostel.com
To:	Rich@RichLucia.com
Subject:	Prospecting and objections
Cc:	

Dad,

What you covered with me about prospecting and going where the business is looks like it pertains to objections, too.

If I go where the business is—and where I'm more apt to be accepted—then I might just face fewer objections, right?

Good idea. But how do I know where the business is?

Alex

From: Rich@RichLucia.com
To: Alex@Intecostel.com
Subject: Michelangelo
Cc:

Alex,

One day, a lady who was totally amazed at young Michelangelo's talent asked him how he carved a man on a horse out of a block of marble. He responded by saying, "It's easy. Just carve away everything that doesn't look like a man on a horse."

Using the "180 Rule," answer this question. Where would you go if you didn't want to meet someone who would buy your product? How about door to door without knowing what's on the other side? How about calling on the companies with the biggest buildings?

Obviously, determining where to go takes a little time to work out, but it's time worth spending. For example, go to that trade show (you know, the one for which you didn't pass out free tickets) and watch who spends the most time at your competitor's booth. That's *your* prospect, too.

Dad

From: Alex@Intecostel.com
To: Rich@RichLucia.com
Subject: Keep trying
Cc:

Dad,

My manager says objections are part of the territory. We have to deal with them and learn all the comebacks. We're told to write down objections and bring them to our meeting. Then we'll figure out, as a group, how to come up with a spin response for each situation.

Alex

From: Rich@RichLucia.com
To: Alex@Intecostel.com
Subject: Objections as excuses
Cc:

Alex,

Sometimes salespeople use objections as excuses. Say you just lost a sale. There must be a reason for it.

You may need an excuse to carry on or not. In any event, you need it so grab it quickly. You have to go back to the office with *something*—if not an order, then at least being able to state a customer objection. It should be an objection right from the prospect's mouth explaining why there was "no sale today."

So we ask the uninterested prospect, "Why not this product? Is there an objection to buying it?" At least we'd have something we could bring back to R&D or our pricing folks. I watched companies change pricing, features, and even their strategy because "so-called objections" never really validated their worth.

A better strategy is to avoid the objections trap *altogether*.

Dad

From: Alex@Intecostel.com
To: Rich@RichLucia.com
Subject: OK, I got it
Cc:

Dad,

What you're saying is that going to the right place will avoid the need to spend a lot of my time handling objections. But what do I do about all the other objection traps?

Alex

From: Rich@RichLucia.com
To: Alex@Intecostel.com
Subject: Four objection traps
Cc:

Alex,

Typically, you can fall into what I call our four objection traps. We've already talked about the first—not going to see people who have no need or willingness to buy your product. You have an Aunt Rosie. I can guarantee that, no matter how hard you pitch her and what objections you overcome with her, she won't buy anything. So why waste your time?

I know, as salespeople, we're taught to hold in the highest esteem the salesperson who could "sell snow to an Eskimo." But that's a myth. If you could find such an Eskimo, he'd realize that, when he got home, he had enough snow and would cancel the order.

Remember, selling is helping others achieve *their* results (pain/gain) while you achieve *your* results (a sale). Make it a win/win scenario. Why? Because no good comes from *forcing* a sale. Why start with an unwilling prospect in the first place?

Dad

From: Alex@Intecostel.com
To: Rich@RichLucia.com
Subject: OK, I'll bite
Cc:

Dad,

What are the other three objections?

Alex

P.S. Are you delaying telling me about them on purpose or are you trying to get me to ask questions?

From: Rich@RichLucia.com
To: Alex@Intecostel.com
Subject: The second objection trap
Cc:

📎 Attachment: Selling a Website

Alex,

Okay. Here it is.

The second objection trap is the objection *you* create.

That's right. YOU!

Experience shows that sixty percent of all prospect objections come from *you*. Salespeople create more monsters or objections in prospects' minds than any other single cause.

We accomplish this by bombarding anyone who will listen with an endless supply of canned pitches, boiler-plate proposals, and one-size-fits-all PowerPoint presentations. Our mission is to place "ideas" in a prospect's head rather than guide the ideas in their heads toward our sales solution. But we insist on pitching when we should be listening. When we are pitching, our prospects are catching—that is, they're catching our words as they apply to the reference points in their heads. While this is happening—bang—an objection is created.

The story in this attachment explains it well. Take a look.

Dad

📎 Selling a Website

A salesperson who represented a website design company received an inquiry from a three-person law firm about creating a website for the firm. If he'd taken the time to explore what the prospect was thinking, he would have found out that the firm had no one on-site who could be the IT technician.

The prospect believed the firm needed a website but didn't want to take time away from his practice to develop and maintain it himself.

However, the salesperson didn't uncover these facts ahead of time. Instead, he arrived with a PowerPoint show to demonstrate how great his company's product was. At this early stage in the sales process, the prospect had not stated any objections. The salesperson began his canned presentation, just as he'd done a hundred times before. With great enthusiasm, he explained how the law firm could customize the look and feel of the websites he showed. Out came the endless samples of fonts, followed by colors, graphics, and clipart—a vast menu for the prospect to choose from.

Next, the salesperson demonstrated how the site could be customized. It included changing content, inserting videos, and using semi-automated HTML coding. Then he gave an overview of how the prospect could monitor and filter email and other mailbox options as the administrator of site.

At that point, the prospect asked, "What's the price for all this?" The salesperson, encouraged by getting this "buy sign" question, went into a twenty-minute list of options, which led to a further description of features. The call ended with a firm handshake from the prospect and a promise to "look over everything and get back to you."

Let's take a look at what happened here. In his haste to show off his project, the salesperson never communicated a direct benefit to the prospect or asked what was important to him. Indeed, he never uncovered the prospect's needs and desires at all!

In football, would a quarterback run into a game without knowing what yard line his team was on? Or what down it is? Or where the opposing team's defense is weak or strong? Then why do salespeople run into their sales game unprepared? And why don't they ask for the very information that will help them avoid creating objections?

In the case of the lawyer, if his "thought bubble" could be seen, it would say, "I have serious concerns about this offering. It's too complex and too time consuming for me. I need to get back to work."

In the meantime, the salesperson figured that the call ended after the pricing conversation. He surmised that "price" must be the prospect's objection to buying that day. Armed with this belief, the salesperson returned to the office and told his manager that if they wanted this sale, they'd better address pricing, perhaps lowering it.

What has this salesperson just done? He made up the fact that the prospect created a price objection, and also ran back to his company communicating it to others!

From: Alex@Intecostel.com
To: Rich@RichLucia.com
Subject: OK—I get the point, Dad
Cc:

Dad,

I just read your attachment and your story makes the point well. So I have to be careful what I say to a prospect. All the time. And I shouldn't make up any objections.

Alex

From: Rich@RichLucia.com
To: Alex@Intecostel.com
Subject: The third objection trap
Cc:

Alex,

Be careful. Not only *what you say* can create an objection, but *everything you do* and *how you market your product* affects the communication, too.

I once did some consulting work for a startup software company. The head of this company was quite proud of an expensive sign hanging outside above the office. Good-looking sign. In fact, he was so proud of that sign that a photo of the outside of the building dominated by that sign became the major presence on its website. But the rather small building was located in a strip mall, and the picture did not depict credibility for their product—a one-million-dollar software product.

That photo itself created an objection that this company might be too small to support a huge software offering, and might not be around in the long haul. This concern was established via a photo on the web without a word being spoken.

Dad

From: Alex@Intecostel.com
To: Rich@RichLucia.com
Subject: The fourth?
Cc:

Dad,

So everything a company puts out affects perceptions that can lead to objections. I see.

What's the fourth objection trap?

Alex

From: Rich@RichLucia.com
To: Alex@Intecostel.com
Subject: The fourth objection trap
Cc:

Alex,

Did you ever notice that people stop trying to find fault with someone they respect? And if they do, they seem to be more open to discuss the issue and help resolve it. That's what listening well and gaining respect do to help you out of the fourth objection trap.

So the fourth objection trap is not listening carefully. I'm not only talking about listening so you understand your prospect's concerns; I'm also talking about listening to gain respect.

When you are respected, you're creditable. Customers will be less willing to pick apart you and your company, and more willing to understand your message.

Dad

From: Alex@Intecostel.com
To: Rich@RichLucia.com
Subject: All ties in
Cc:

Dad,

I'm guessing this stuff is all interrelated. I realized that prospecting, questioning, and listening were important on their own, but I can see how they can all serve me well in the objection area.

This objection stuff is fragile, like walking on eggs.

Alex

From: Rich@RichLucia.com
To: Alex@Intecostel.com
Subject: Walking on eggs
Cc:

 Attachment: Objections

Alex,

At this point in the sales process, you probably believe that everything you say and do has an effect on creating objections. Well, you're partially right. Everything you say and do *does* affect your success. But walking on eggs is something you *choose* to do. You *always* have a choice.

If you're willing to continue to only "handle objections," go ahead and step about freely. If you land on a couple of eggshells, you can attempt damage control and handle the objection with one of a thousand pre-spun phrases. But if you're truly interested in avoiding the hassle, your time will be better spent avoiding the objection traps in the first place.

See how I've summarized these four objections in this attachment.

Dad

Objections

Avoid these four objection traps

1. Go where people want and have a need for your product. Chip away everything that doesn't look like a customer.

2. Don't make up objections that aren't there.

3. Be careful how you present yourself.

4. Listen closely to build trust.

*"**Handling**" objections can be too messy, too late, and too time wasting. Instead, learn to avoid **objections**.*

Almost the Decision Maker

From: Alex@Intecostel.com
To: Rich@RichLucia.com
Subject: Red flag revisited
Cc:

Dad,

A while back when I told you my prospect needed to know about my competition, you said something about a red flag—that I might not be dealing with the decision maker.

What did you mean by that?

Alex

From: Rich@RichLucia.com
To: Alex@Intecostel.com
Subject: Decision maker
Cc:

Alex,

Whenever someone says he or she has to put together a comparison chart, immediately ask, "For whom?" That's a sign that someone else, not the person you are talking to, will make the buying decision.

No respectful sales training manual would say anything other than this: "You have to deal with the decision maker." And that is so true.

However, "Selling in the NOW" tells us that frequently the decision maker has delegated the responsibility or is not available all the time. So what do you do? "Walk away," assert sales trainers of yesteryear. "If you can't deal with the decision maker, then don't deal at all."

Wise words for the past. But today, you might not have a choice. Good salespeople try their best to get a good hand to play. But after all is said and done, they have to play the cards they are dealt—which could mean no direct access to the top.

Dad

From: Alex@Intecostel.com
To: Rich@RichLucia.com
Subject: I try
Cc:

Dad,

I always try to reach the decision maker, but you're right, sometimes it's tough. The person who eventually signs doesn't want to participate in the decision-making process. Delegating becomes a way out.

I don't want "empowerment" to force me out of the game.

Alex

From: Rich@RichLucia.com
To: Alex@Intecostel.com
Subject: Empowerment
Cc:

Alex,

You're right, son. Some people hide being lazy behind the "empowerment" card, but either way, we don't always get to talk with the decision maker.

If you don't have access, you have choices. You can:

- *Pack up and move on.*
- *Keep trying to get to the decision maker.*
- *Play the cards you've been dealt and work with the decision maker's delegate.*

I'm not big on giving up and moving on, especially when I've already qualified an opportunity as being strong. You can always use the tool we call "NEXT DOOR."

Dad

From:	Alex@Intecostel.com
To:	Rich@RichLucia.com
Subject:	No NEXT DOOR for me
Cc:	

Dad,

I'm with ya, Dad. I've been on calls where I know they are in the process of making a decision for a solution my product can offer, but I can't get to the decision maker. I don't want to walk away.

Got any ideas?

Alex

From: Rich@RichLucia.com
To: Alex@Intecostel.com
Subject: Moving up the food chain
Cc:

Alex,

You can usually find ways to get to the decision maker through a decision "influencer"—someone on staff who can influence the outcome.

First, use your questioning skills to find out not only what the company's pain is, but also what this influencer can gain. Then ask why this "pain" factor is important to the decision maker. You'll find this information useful after you've gained the respect of the influencer.

You can ask the influencer questions that only the decision maker can answer, which could get you a ticket to see that person. Or you can show empathy for the influencer and give a compliment on how the project has been handled thus far. Then suggest setting up a breakfast, lunch, or short meeting with the decision maker and the equivalent titleholder from your own company. Explain that the two managers can relate well to each other and move the project along. Promise that this meeting of executives won't be too time-consuming.

Dad

From: Alex@Intecostel.com
To: Rich@RichLucia.com
Subject: Sounds like a plan
Cc:

Dad,

If all that doesn't work, what's next? How else can I play with those cards?

Alex

From: Rich@RichLucia.com
To: Alex@Intecostel.com
Subject: Play those cards
Cc:

Alex,

To stay in the game, you have to realize you're "Selling in the NOW" to the decision influencers. And they also operate in the now. Play to the fact that most are dedicated, but not *obsessed* with their jobs and their projects, especially if they're Gen Xers. They have other motivations, so find out what they are early on.

Specifically, ask what's expected of them and what they believe the decision maker wants as a final recommendation or report. Keep in mind they're intent on getting information of value to the decision maker, not necessarily to choose the best solution themselves. Once you find out what their desired "deliverable" would look like, help them create that report or recommendation. Better still, do it for them.

Dad

From: Alex@Intecostel.com
To: Rich@RichLucia.com
Subject: Write their reports for them?
Cc:

Dad,

You want me to write their report for them? They will *never* go for that.

Alex

From:	Rich@RichLucia.com
To:	Alex@Intecostel.com
Subject:	Depends on how you do it
Cc:	

Alex,

This is where you have to take great care. Listen carefully regarding what is expected of them and what deliverable will achieve their gain.

If you've found out their pain and gain, then you will know what will motivate them to allow you to assist. For now, the "sale" you want to make is to let as much of your influence reach the final decision maker.

Here are a few tips. All information you provide and any comparison charts regarding you and your competition should be done on plain paper, no letterhead. They should speak about your company in the third person (as if the influencer wrote it, not you). Be sure to give an electronic version of the report to the influencer. (As you know, cutting and pasting a document on the computer is very easy.) Most prospects or influencers appreciate this kind of help so they can give their attention to other motivations.

Dad

From: Alex@Intecostel.com
To: Rich@RichLucia.com
Subject: I can do that
Cc:

Dad,

Does that really work? Is it as good as dealing with the decision maker directly?

Alex

From:	Rich@RichLucia.com
To:	Alex@Intecostel.com
Subject:	No way
Cc:	
📎	Attachment: Influencing the Decision Influencer

Alex,

Again, dealing with the decision maker is always the best route to go. However, if you can't, it beats walking away from the opportunity.

Buying decisions are made by salespeople engaged with the decision maker. What we're doing here is getting the odds in your favor when the situation comes up.

Remember, always make your influencers aware that you're working for *their* gain. Then they'll be more inclined to get you an audience with the decision maker (who also controls their gain) whenever they can.

Dad

This attachment summarizes what you can do.

Influencing the Decision Influencer

When you have a true opportunity in hand and you are not calling on the decision maker, take these three steps:

5. *Try your best to get to the decision maker, but don't walk away.*

6. *Ask questions to understand the decision influencer's pain and gain.*

7. *Assist the decision influencer's task any way you can.*

Use the "180 Rule": What would I do if I didn't want the correct information to get back to the decision maker?

From: Alex@Intecostel.com
To: Rich@RichLucia.com
Subject: Lotta stuff
Cc:

Dad,

I've been keeping all your emails in a folder and, I've gotta tell you, it's getting pretty big. At least I can look at the ideas again if I get off track.

Alex

From: Rich@RichLucia.com
To: Alex@Intecostel.com
Subject: Good Idea
Cc:

Alex,

I'm glad you are saving the emails, but what's more important is to create your own folder. Seeing what works and doesn't work for you is most important. What I have given you are guidelines you can follow to master your own efforts—your own best practices.

Dad

From: Alex@Intecostel.com
To: Rich@RichLucia.com
Subject: Information
Cc:

Dad,

We installed a new CRM package last week and it's a pain in the neck. We have to write down *everything* about the customer—name, contact numbers, sales call history, etc. My manager checks it every day and I get a nasty e-mail, if I don't fill things out properly.

Some of the other sales people already figured out that bad breath is better than no breath at all, so they're just putting anything down in their reports.

Alex

From: Rich@RichLucia.com
To: Alex@Intecostel.com
Subject: I'm Good!
Cc:

Alex,

You know, your CRM package is really a valuable tool and you should make every attempt to use it to the max (and not just fill it out to satisfy your manager).

Unfortunately, the people who developed these tools are not necessarily sales people. They are detailed organizers who believe that the more detail, the more value. Most salespeople are not detail-oriented, so it's a ying-yang thing. Too often, the ying wins.

So do your best to capture as much information about the companies and the individuals you call on, and sell to meet this requirement. Don't sweat it.

Keep in mind. The value is using the information and not just collecting it.

Dad

From: Alex@Intecostel.com
To: Rich@RichLucia.com
Subject: Loss reports
Cc:

Dad,

Every time we lose a deal, we have to fill out this huge loss report. We then go over these reports in a sales meeting and determine what went wrong and what we could do better in the future.

It has gotten to the point where not only do I feel badly when I lose, but I feel as though I am being punished by having to come up with a reason for my defeat. It rubs salt in a wound. I don't like reliving the pain!

Alex

From: Rich@RichLucia.com
To: Alex@Intecostel.com
Subject: Loss reports
Cc:

Alex,

I understand the thought process behind a loss report, but that was "then" thinking, not "NOW" thinking. It's based on the theory that you can learn from your mistakes, but the reality is that most sales people might never know why they really lost. So what happens? The loss report becomes an excuse bucket.

The truth is that if you truly knew why you were losing a sale, you would do something *not* to lose. No team plays a full game until the final buzzer sounds and then looks up at the scoreboard to see who won.

You have to come home with something, so you find an excuse. Generally, it's not your fault because the decision maker's brother got the sale, or your price was too high, or the prospect liked the incumbent and didn't want to change.

Loss reports are excuse buckets that can be accurate, but they're rarely helpful.

Dad

From: Alex@Intecostel.com
To: Rich@RichLucia.com
Subject: What's now?
Cc:

Dad,

If loss reports are something from "then," what goes on "NOW"? Win reports?

Alex

From: Rich@RichLucia.com
To: Alex@Intecostel.com
Subject: Win reports
Cc:

Alex,

Yep. You got it. Win reports. So much more can be learned by understanding why and how you won, rather than providing an excuse for why you lost.

After you close the deal and product installation has begun, ask your customers why they bought from you and what was right about your product. You'll learn more about what you did right, and more about the kind of customer and situation that will lead to another sale. It will also help you develop an ideal customer profile so you can know where to hunt for another sale.

More than that, you'll find out what the competition did wrong. That way, you can learn a good "bad" example that has really happened.

Finding out what you did right will reinforce your skills while making it easier to find more of the same type of customer. Also, it will give you a more meaningful reference.

Dad

From:	Alex@Intecostel.com
To:	Rich@RichLucia.com
Subject:	I love it
Cc:	

Dad,

Thanks, I love it. A win report. It makes a lot of sense.

You know, Dad, we have plenty of customers who've already bought our product. I know that no one in the office really knows *why* their customers bought or what value they are getting from our product.

Alex

From: Rich@RichLucia.com
To: Alex@Intecostel.com
Subject: That's too bad
Cc:

Alex,

So many salespeople look every day for the silver bullet that will bring down all the elephants. Sometimes they don't realize that the answers are right under their noses.

You will find a lot of "bad" examples that make good learning experiences as you go through your selling career. Focus on taking the course that's best for your customers *and* for you.

Remember, if you want to earn in the upper two percent of the population, you'll have to do something different than ninety-eight percent of your peers.

But never forget, you can only be good at something if you have a desire and a passion for what you do. Earning money will come; it's the natural reward as you travel the road. Remember what I told you early on: there's no meaningful journey without integrity, customer caring, understanding human nature, and a love for solving people's problems.

Unless, of course, this whole "Selling in the NOW" thing is too tough for you. Constantly learning and practicing your skills takes time and effort. In retrospect, power washing decks looked like it could be a fun career!

Dad

From: Alex@Intecostel.com
To: Rich@RichLucia.com
Subject: Power washing decks
Cc:

Dad,

Forget power washing. I love this job, Dad. You were right. Selling is a great career. Thanks again for all your help.

BTW, what would you have said to me if you didn't want me to stay in sales?

Alex

Printed in the United States
102799LV00002B/139-498/P